Pip Met Bun

By Sally Cowan

Pip gets in the pit
and naps.

Tam runs to see Pip.

Pip sits up.

He can see Bun in the bag.

It is **my** pit!
It is not Bun's pit.

Pip is mad at Tam.

He hops to the pots.

Hop, hop, hop!

Pip hid in a big pot.

Pip can see Tam pat Bun.

Pip is sad.

But Bun gets up.

Bun hops to the big pot!

Pip met Bun at the big pot!

Pip and Bun ran to the pit.

Pip and Bun go
hop, hop, hop!

It is fun!

CHECKING FOR MEANING

1. Where did Pip hide? *(Literal)*

2. Why was Pip sad? *(Literal)*

3. Why did Bun hop to the big pot? *(Inferential)*

EXTENDING VOCABULARY

bag	What is a *bag*? Look at the word. What new word would you make if you took away the *g* and put a *t* at the end?
sad	What does it mean to feel *sad*? What makes you feel *sad*? What other words do you know that describe how you feel? E.g. happy, excited, lonely, scared.
fun	Find a word in the story that rhymes with *fun*. Which letters are the same? Which letter is different? What things do you do that are *fun*?

MOVING BEYOND THE TEXT

1. Why do animals sometimes behave differently when a new pet joins the family?

2. How would or did you feel if or when you had a new baby brother or sister?

3. What are some of the reasons animals hide when they are in the wild?

4. Why is it helpful for Pip to have another rabbit to play with?

SPEED SOUNDS

Dd	Jj	Oo	Gg	Uu

Cc	Bb	Rr	Ee	Ff	Hh	Nn

Mm	Ss	Aa	Pp	Ii	Tt

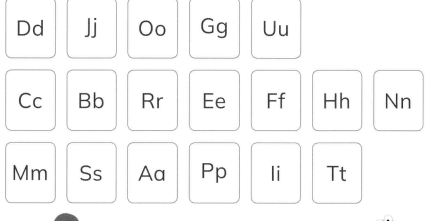

PRACTICE WORDS

gets

runs

Bun

bag

not

mad

But

hops

pots

hop

sad

and

hid

Hop

fun

big

pot

up